God's Precious Promises on Healing

By

Leslie J. Kimbro

ISBN: 1-4033-1333-4 (e-book)
ISBN: 1-40331-334-2 (Paperback)

This book is printed on acid free paper.

1st Books - rev. 07/09/02

God's Precious Promises on Healing

Leslie J. Kimbro

Daily Living In The Word Of God Ministries, Inc.
P.O. Box 310959
Atlanta, GA 31131-0959

Unless otherwise indicated, all scripture quotations are taken from the King James Version of the Bible. Copyright © 1976 by Thomas Nelson, Inc. Nashville, TN Printed in the Republic of Korea

Scipture marked Amplified (or AMP) are scripture taken from the Amplified Bible, Expanded Edition. Copyright © 1987 by the Zondervan Corporation and Lockman Foundation. All rights reserved. Printed in the United States of America

Professional Editing Services by:
Bonita Watts
Cornucopia Diversified
(404) 449-3043
bswatts@myexel.com

ACKNOWLEDGEMENTS

I thank each volunteer for your persistent and consistent spirit of excellence in helping to fulfill the vision of Daily Living In The Word Of God Ministries. May God continue to richly bless and prosper each of you. May you continue to walk in divine health. I love and appreciate each one of you.

I thank God for Rhema Bible Correspondence School. I will always be grateful to Brother **Kenneth Hagin Sr**. for teaching the principles of Healing with simplicity and understanding.

Janet Lucas, Deirdre Jackson, Bonita Watts, and **Curtis Kimbro,** thank you all so much for your sacrifice of time in typing and editing this book.

Barbara Watkins and **Delores Wynne**, I thank you for your loyalty and support. Your spirit of excellence continues to encourage me to push higher.

Deirdra Yarbrough, I thank you for your love and support in helping to make this project a success.

Without all of your help, and the help of many others, this book would not be available. My prayer is that this book will benefit and encourage all who read it to press towards the mark for the prize of the high calling. As long as you don't quit, cave in, or give up, you will receive the victory.

DEDICATION

Dedicated to my wonderful husband Curtis and the DLWGM volunteer staff.

I will always be grateful for your patience, love, support, and understanding the call of God on my life.

TABLE OF CONTENTS

VISION

Daily Living In The Word Of God Ministries, Inc., is an evangelistic outreach ministry commissioned to carry the Gospel of Jesus Christ throughout the nations. We are dedicated and committed to helping lost souls meet Jesus, and begin their relationship with Him.

Our vision: To teach all to spend *__daily__* time with Jesus Christ in order to establish a personal relationship with him; and to teach that the healing power of Jesus Christ is available to all who believe and act on the Word of God.

I have been anointed by God to start an **INTERNATIONAL HEALING SCHOOL**. The objective for starting this international healing school is to teach the children of God that they have authority over the devil. I want the Body of Christ to know that there is nothing terminal with God. It does not matter what the diagnosis is.

From a simple cold to cancer, if a person is willing to apply the word of God as instructed, a harvest of divine health will be the end result.

God desires for His children to walk in divine health all the days of their lives. He said in Psalm 91:16, "With long life will I satisfy him, and show him my salvation." God desires for each of His children to live a long, healthy, and prosperous life. My responsibility is to teach that in consistency lies the breakthrough! One must be consistent and persistent about the things of God. As long as you don't quit, cave in, or give up, you will receive the victory—a harvest of divine health.

I have been commissioned by God to take this International Healing School around the world. If you cannot come to us, we will bring the International Healing School to you. My responsibility is to teach you how to use your God-given authority through the power of confession. **The Word of God is our defense**. Ephesians 6:11 tells us to "Put on the whole armour of God, that ye may be able to stand against the wiles of the devil." Psalms 91:4 (The Living Bible) tells us, "…His faithful promises are your armor." When we take the time to daily clothe ourselves in the armor of God's Word through the power of confession, no sickness, disease, poverty, lack, debt, or any other curse can remain in our lives. The circumstances and situations must change to line up with God's Word, because God said in Isaiah 55:11, "My word…shall not return unto me void."

In addition to the Healing School, I also teach a weekly class entitled, **"ABIDING IN HIS PRESENCE**." St. John 15:7 says, "If ye abide in me, and my words abide in you, ye shall ask what ye will, and it shall be done unto you." The objective of this class is to teach the saints that everything we need is found in the presence of the

Lord. The key to it all is that we must <u>abide in His presence</u> in order to get every need met and have every prayer answered. Everything we need and desire to have is found in the presence of the Lord.

I encourage you today to take control of the circumstances in your life through the power of confession and abiding in the presence of the Lord.

AUTHOR'S TESTIMONY

Sometimes in life what happens is that our testimony becomes our ministry. That is what happened in my life. To give you a brief version of my testimony, I am a lady who, in 1996-1997, could barely put one foot in front of the other. Satan had attacked my body with a disease called Myastenia-Gravis. This disease attacks your immune system, and it takes away all of your strength. Literally, everything had to be done for me. I had to be bathed, my teeth had to be brushed, and I had to be clothed. As I said, I could barely put one foot in front of the other.

I called on the only One I knew, who was Jesus my Savior. Prior to this sickness, I had done a 6-year intense study in the Word of God under brother Kenneth Hagin from Rhema Bible Correspondence School in the area of healing. I had always been fascinated at how a word could be so powerful that it could affect the physical body. When the attack came, I ran straight to the Father; He told me, "It is already inside of you what you need to do. *Now, it is time for execution.*"

I cooperated with the natural while applying the supernatural. I went through surgery. My doctor's main concern was whether or not my total strength could be restored. From that point, I knew it was between me and the Father. I found every healing and strength scripture in the Bible from Genesis to Revelation. I began pouring that Word into my spirit (through the power of confession) like there were no tomorrow. I stood on God's Word for 18 months. Today, I am a woman who believed the Word, applied the Word, and reaped a 100-fold harvest. The Word of God works when we work the Word.

My reason for writing this book is to teach you that there is nothing terminal with God. We have authority over the devil through the blood of Jesus. The authority we have is exercised through the words we speak. If you are willing to confess the Word of God in the face of disease, sickness, debt, poverty and any other curse, you will come out on top, possessing exactly what the Word says you can have—victory!

It has been my pleasure to write this book as a vehicle to guide you into the fulfillment of the promises of God.

To God be the glory!

Minister Leslie J. Kimbro

INTRODUCTION

Hello child of God. It is my pleasure to present this book to you entitled: *God's Precious Promises on Healing.* I have created this book to feed your Spirit-man the Word of God in the area of healing. Child of God, it does not matter what the diagnosis is. Whether it is a cold or cancer, the healing power of Jesus Christ will remove it, and heal you of that infirmity. When Jesus went to the cross for your sins, He also took your sickness, disease and pain. Romans 10:17 tells us that *faith comes by us hearing the word of God.* It is my desire that you will meditate and confess these scriptures continually by feeding your spirit man these faith-filled promises from the anointed Word of God. As you do, meditate and confess these scriptures, and expect to be healed in the Name of Jesus.

GOD'S PRECIOUS PROMISES ON HEALING

OLD TESTAMENT

Genesis 20:17

So Abraham prayed unto God: and God healed Abimelech, and his wife, and his maidservants; and they bare children.

Exodus 15:26

And said, If thou wilt diligently hearken to the voice of the LORD thy God, and wilt do that which is right in his sight, and wilt give ear to his commandments, and keep all his statutes, I will put none of these diseases upon thee, which I have brought upon the Egyptians: for I am the LORD that healeth thee.

1

Exodus 23:25-26

And ye shall serve the LORD your God, and he shall bless thy bread, and thy water; and I will take sickness away from the midst of thee. There shall nothing cast their young, nor be barren, in thy land: the number of thy days I will fulfil.

Numbers 23:19

God is not a man, that he should lie; neither the son of man, that he should repent: hath he said, and shall he not do it? or hath he spoken, and shall he not make it good?

Deuteronomy 5:33

Ye shall walk in all the ways which the LORD your God hath commanded you, that ye may live, and that it may be well with you, and that ye may prolong your days in the land which ye shall possess.

Deuteronomy 7:11-15

Thou shalt therefore keep the commandments, and the statutes, and the judgments, which I command thee this day, to do them. Wherefore it shall come to pass, if ye hearken to these judgments, and keep, and do them, that the LORD thy God shall keep unto thee the covenant and the mercy which he sware unto thy fathers: And he will love thee, and bless thee, and multiply thee: he will also bless the fruit of thy womb, and the fruit of thy land, thy corn, and thy wine, and thine oil, the increase of thy kine, and the flocks of thy sheep, in the land which he sware unto thy fathers to give thee. Thou shalt be blessed above all people: there shall not be male or female barren among you, or among your cattle. And the LORD will take away from thee all sickness, and will put none of the evil diseases of Egypt, which thou knowest, upon thee; but will lay them upon all them that hate thee.

3

Deuteronomy 30:19-20

I call heaven and earth to record this day against you, that I have set before you life and death, blessing and cursing: therefore choose life, that both thou and thy seed may live: That thou mayest love the LORD thy God, and that thou mayest obey his voice, and that thou mayest cleave unto him: for he is thy life, and the length of thy days: that thou mayest dwell in the land which the LORD sware unto thy fathers, to Abraham, to Isaac, and to Jacob, to give them.

I Kings 8:56

Blessed be the LORD, that hath given rest unto his people Israel, according to all that he promised: there hath not failed one word of all his good promise, which he promised by the hand of Moses his servant.

Psalms 30:2

O LORD my God, I cried unto thee, and thou hast healed me.

Psalms 34:19

Many are the afflictions of the righteous: but the LORD delivereth him out of them all.

Psalms 41:3

The LORD will strengthen him upon the bed of languishing: thou wilt make all his bed in his sickness.

(AMPLIFIED) The Lord will sustain, refresh, and strengthen him on his bed of languishing: all his bed You [O Lord] will turn, change, and transform in his illness.

Psalms 91:9-10, 14-16

Because thou hast made the LORD, which is my refuge, even the most High, thy habitation; There shall no evil befall thee, neither shall any plague come nigh thy dwelling.

Because he hath set his love upon me, therefore will I deliver him: I will set him on high, because he hath known my name. He shall call upon me, and I will answer him: I will be with him in trouble; I will deliver him, and honour him. With long life will I satisfy him, and show him my salvation.

Psalms 103:1-5

Bless the LORD, O my soul: and all that is within me, bless his holy name. Bless the LORD, O my soul, and forget not all his benefits: Who forgiveth all thine iniquities; who healeth all thy diseases;

Who redeemeth thy life from destruction; who crowneth thee with loving kindness and tender mercies;

Who satisfieth thy mouth with good things; so that thy youth is renewed like the eagle's.

Psalms 105:37

He brought them forth also with silver and gold: and there was not one feeble person among their tribes.

Psalms 107:19-21

Then they cry unto the LORD in their trouble, and he saveth them out of their distresses.

He sent his word, and healed them, and delivered them from their destructions. Oh that men would praise the LORD for his goodness, and for his wonderful works to the children of men!

Psalms 118:17

I shall not die, but live, and declare the works of the LORD.

Psalms 147:3

He healeth the broken in heart, and bindeth up their wounds. **(AMPLIFIED)** He heals the brokenhearted and binds up their wounds [curing their pains and their sorrows].

Proverbs 3:1-2

My son, forget not my law; but let thine heart keep my commandments: For length of days, and long life, and peace, shall they add to thee. **(AMPLIFIED)** My son forget not my law or teaching, but let your heart keep my commandments; For length of days and years of a life [worth living] and tranquility [inward and outward and continuing through old age till death] these shall they add to you.

Proverbs 3:7-8

Be not wise in thine own eyes: fear the LORD, and depart from evil. It shall be health to thy navel, and marrow to thy bones. **(AMPLIFIED)** Be not wise in your own eyes; reverently fear and worship the Lord and turn [entirely] away from evil. It shall be health to your nerves and sinews, and marrow and moistening to your bones.

Proverbs 4:20-24

My son, attend to my words; incline thine ear unto my sayings. Let them not depart from thine eyes; keep them in the midst of thine heart. For they are life unto those that find them, and health to all their flesh. Keep thy heart with all diligence; for out of it are the issues of life. Put away from

9

thee a froward mouth, and perverse lips put far from thee. **(AMPLIFIED)** My son, attend to my words; consent and submit to my sayings. Let them not depart from your sight; keep them in the center of your heart. For they are life to those who find them, healing and health to all their flesh. Keep and guard your heart with all vigilance and above all that you guard for out of it flow the springs of life. Put away from you false and dishonest speech, and willful and contrary talk put far from you.

Proverbs 9:11

For by me thy days shall be multiplied, and the years of thy life shall be increased.

Proverbs 14:30

A sound heart is the life of the flesh: but envy the rottenness of the bones.

(AMPLIFIED) A calm and undisturbed mind and heart are the life and health of the body, but envy, jealousy, and wrath are like rottenness of the bones.

Proverbs 16:24

Pleasant words are as an honeycomb, sweet to the soul, and health to the bones.

Isaiah 40:29, 31

He giveth power to the faint; and to them that have no might he increaseth strength.

But they that wait upon the LORD shall renew their strength; they shall mount up with wings as eagles; they shall run, and not be weary; and they shall walk, and not faint.

Isaiah 41:10, 13

Fear thou not; for I am with thee: be not dismayed; for I am thy God: I will strengthen thee;

yea, I will help thee; yea, I will uphold thee with the right hand of my righteousness.

For I the LORD thy God will hold thy right hand, saying unto thee, Fear not; I will help thee.

Isaiah 53:4-5

Surely he hath borne our griefs, and carried our sorrows: yet we did esteem him stricken, smitten of God, and afflicted. But he was wounded for our transgressions, he was bruised for our iniquities: the chastisement of our peace was upon him; and with his stripes we are healed.

Isaiah 55:11

So shall my word be that goeth forth out of my mouth: it shall not return unto me void, but it shall accomplish that which I please, and it shall prosper in the thing whereto I sent it.

Isaiah 58:8

Then shall thy light break forth as the morning, and thine health shall spring forth speedily: and thy righteousness shall go before thee; the glory of the LORD shall be thy rearward. **(AMPLIFIED)** Then shall your light break forth like the morning and your healing (your restoration and the power of a new life) shall spring forth speedily, your righteousness (your rightness, your justice, and your right relationship with God) shall go before you [conducting you to peace and prosperity], and the glory of the Lord shall be your rear guard.

Jeremiah 1:12

Then said the LORD unto me, Thou hast well seen: for I will hasten my word to perform it.

Jeremiah 17:14

Heal me, O LORD, and I shall be healed; save me, and I shall be saved: for thou art my praise.

Jeremiah 30:17

For I will restore health unto thee, and I will heal thee of thy wounds, saith the LORD; because they called thee an Outcast, saying, This is Zion, whom no man seeketh after.

Joel 3:10

Beat your plowshares into swords, and your pruning hooks into spears: let the weak say, I am strong.

Nahum 1:7, 9

The LORD is good, a strong hold in the day of trouble; and he knoweth them that trust in him.

What do ye imagine against the LORD? he will make an utter end: affliction shall not rise up the second time.

Malachi 3:6

For I am the LORD, I change not; therefore ye sons of Jacob are not consumed.

Malachi 4:2

But unto you that fear my name shall the Sun of righteousness arise with healing in his wings; and ye shall go forth, and grow up as calves of the stall.

Leslie J. Kimbro

GOD'S PRECIOUS PROMISES ON HEALING

NEW TESTAMENT

Matthew 4:23-24

And Jesus went about all Galilee, teaching in their synagogues, and preaching the gospel of the kingdom, and healing all manner of sickness and all manner of disease among the people.

And his fame went throughout all Syria: and they brought unto him all sick people that were taken with divers diseases and torments, and those which were possessed with devils, and those which were lunatic, and those that had the palsy; and he healed them.

Matthew 8:2-3

And, behold, there came a leper and worshipped him, saying, Lord, if thou wilt, thou canst make me clean. And Jesus put forth his hand, and touched him, saying, I will; be thou clean. And immediately his leprosy was cleansed.

Matthew 8:5-10, 13

And when Jesus was entered into Capernaum, there came unto him a centurion, beseeching him,

And saying, Lord, my servant lieth at home sick of the palsy, grievously tormented. And Jesus saith unto him, I will come and heal him. The centurion answered and said, Lord, I am not worthy that thou shouldest come under my roof: but speak the word only, and my servant shall be healed. For I am a man under authority, having soldiers under me: and I say to this man, Go, and he goeth; and to another, Come, and he cometh;

17

and to my servant, Do this, and he doeth it. When Jesus heard it, he marvelled, and said to them that followed, Verily I say unto you, I have not found so great faith, no, not in Israel. And Jesus said unto the centurion, Go thy way; and as thou hast believed, so be it done unto thee. And his servant was healed in the selfsame hour.

Matthew 8:14-17

And when Jesus was come into Peter's house, he saw his wife's mother laid, and sick of a fever. And he touched her hand, and the fever left her: and she arose, and ministered unto them. When the even was come, they brought unto him many that were possessed with devils: and he cast out the spirits with his word, and healed all that were sick: That it might be fulfilled which was spoken by Esaias the prophet, saying, Himself took our infirmities, and bare our sicknesses. **(AMPLIFIED)** And thus He fulfilled what was spoken by the prophet Isaiah, He Himself took [in order to carry away] our weaknesses and infirmities and bore away our diseases.

Matthew 9:20-22, 27-29

And, behold, a woman, which was diseased with an issue of blood twelve years, came behind him, and touched the hem of his garment: For she said within herself, If I may but touch his garment, I shall be whole. But Jesus turned him about, and when he saw her, he said, Daughter, be of good comfort; thy faith hath made thee whole. And the woman was made whole from that hour.

And when Jesus departed thence, two blind men followed him, crying, and saying, Thou Son of David, have mercy on us. And when he was come into the house, the blind men came to him: and Jesus saith unto them, Believe ye that I am able to do this? They said unto him, Yea, Lord.

Then touched he their eyes, saying, According to your faith be it unto you.

Matthew 10:7-8

And as ye go, preach, saying, The kingdom of heaven is at hand. Heal the sick, cleanse the lepers, raise the dead, cast out devils: freely ye have received, freely give.

Matthew 11:2-5

Now when John had heard in the prison the works of Christ, he sent two of his disciples, And said unto him, Art thou he that should come, or do we look for another? Jesus answered and said unto them, Go and show John again those things which ye do hear and see: The blind receive their sight, and the lame walk, the lepers are cleansed, and the deaf hear, the dead are raised up, and the poor have the gospel preached to them.

Matthew 12:15

But when Jesus knew it, he withdrew himself from thence: and great multitudes followed him, and he healed them all;

Matthew 14:13-14, 34-36

When Jesus heard of it, he departed thence by ship into a desert place apart: and when the people had heard thereof, they followed him on foot out of the cities. And Jesus went forth, and saw a great multitude, and was moved with compassion toward them, and he healed their sick.

And when they were gone over, they came into the land of Gennesaret. And when the men of that place had knowledge of him, they sent out into all that country round about, and brought unto him all that were diseased; And besought him that they might only touch the hem of his garment: and as many as touched were made perfectly whole.

Matthew 15:29-31

And Jesus departed from thence, and came nigh unto the sea of Galilee; and went up into a mountain, and sat down there. And great multitudes came unto him, having with them those that were lame, blind, dumb, maimed, and many others, and cast them down at Jesus' feet; and he healed them:

Insomuch that the multitude wondered, when they saw the dumb to speak, the maimed to be whole, the lame to walk, and the blind to see: and they glorified the God of Israel.

Matthew 18:18-19

Verily I say unto you, Whatsoever ye shall bind on earth shall be bound in heaven: and whatsoever ye shall loose on earth shall be loosed in heaven. Again I say unto you, That if two of you shall agree on earth as touching any thing that they shall ask, it shall be done for them of my Father which is in heaven.

Matthew 19:1-2

And it came to pass, that when Jesus had finished these sayings, he departed from Galilee, and came into the coasts of Judaea beyond Jordan; And great multitudes followed him; and he healed them there.

Matthew 21:14, 21-22

And the blind and the lame came to him in the temple; and he healed them.

Jesus answered and said unto them, Verily I say unto you, If ye have faith, and doubt not, ye shall not only do this which is done to the fig tree, but also if ye shall say unto this mountain, Be thou removed, and be thou cast into the sea; it shall be done. And all things, whatsoever ye shall ask in prayer, believing, ye shall receive.

Matthew 24:35

Heaven and earth shall pass away, but my words shall not pass away.

Mark 1:32-34

And at even, when the sun did set, they brought unto him all that were diseased, and them that were possessed with devils. And all the city was gathered together at the door. And he healed many that were sick of divers diseases, and cast out many devils; and suffered not the devils to speak, because they knew him.

Mark 2:1-12

And again he entered into Capernaum, after some days; and it was noised that he was in the house.

And straightway many were gathered together, insomuch that there was no room to receive them, no, not so much as about the door: and he preached the word unto them. And they come unto him, bringing one sick of the palsy, which was borne of four. And when they could not come nigh unto him for the press, they uncovered the roof where he was: and when they had broken it up, they let down the bed wherein the sick of the palsy lay. When Jesus saw their faith, he said unto the sick of the palsy, Son, thy sins be forgiven thee. But there were certain of the scribes sitting there, and reasoning in their hearts, Why doth this man thus speak blasphemies? who can forgive sins but God only? And immediately when Jesus perceived in his spirit that they so reasoned within themselves, he said unto them, Why reason ye these things in your hearts? Whether is it easier to say to the sick of the palsy, Thy sins be forgiven thee; or to say, Arise, and take up thy bed, and walk? But that ye may know that the Son of man hath power on earth to forgive sins, (he saith to the sick of the palsy,) I say unto thee, Arise, and take up thy bed, and go thy way into thine house. And immediately he arose, took up the bed, and went forth before them all; insomuch that they were all amazed, and glorified God, saying, We never saw it on this fashion.

Mark 3:7-10

But Jesus withdrew himself with his disciples to the sea: and a great multitude from Galilee followed him, and from Judaea, And from Jerusalem, and from Idumaea, and from beyond Jordan; and they about Tyre and Sidon, a great multitude, when they had heard what great things he did, came unto him. And he spake to his disciples, that a small ship should wait on him because of the multitude, lest they should throng him. For he had healed many; insomuch that they pressed upon him for to touch him, as many as had plagues.

Mark 5:21-43

And when Jesus was passed over again by ship unto the other side, much people gathered unto him: and he was nigh unto the sea. And, behold, there cometh one of the rulers of the synagogue, Jairus by name; and when he saw him, he fell at his feet, And besought him greatly, saying, My little daughter lieth at the point of death: I pray thee, come and lay thy hands on her, that she may be healed; and she shall live. And Jesus went with him; and much people followed him, and thronged him. And a certain woman, which had an issue of blood twelve years, And had suffered many things of many physicians, and had spent all that she had, and was nothing bettered, but rather grew worse, When she had heard of Jesus, came in the press behind, and touched his garment. For she said, If I may touch but his clothes, I shall be whole. And straightway the fountain of her blood was dried up; and she felt in her body that she was healed of that plague. And Jesus, immediately knowing in himself that virtue had gone out of him, turned him about in the press, and said, Who touched my clothes? And his disciples said unto him, Thou seest the multitude thronging thee, and sayest thou, Who touched me? And he looked round about to see her that had done this thing. But the woman fearing and trembling, knowing what was done in her, came and fell down before him, and told him all the truth. And he said unto her, Daughter, thy faith hath made thee whole; go in peace, and be whole of thy plague. While he yet spake, there came from the ruler of the synagogue's house certain which said, Thy daughter is dead: why troublest thou the Master any further? As soon as Jesus heard the word that was spoken, he saith unto the ruler of the synagogue, Be not afraid, only believe. And he suffered no man to follow him, save Peter, and James, and John the brother of James. And he cometh to the house of the ruler of the synagogue, and seeth the tumult, and them that wept and wailed greatly. And when he was come in, he saith unto them, Why make ye this ado, and weep? the damsel is not dead, but sleepeth. And they laughed him to scorn. But when he had put them all out, he taketh the father and the mother of the damsel, and them that were with him, and entereth in where the damsel was lying. And he took the damsel by the hand, and said unto her, Talitha cumi; which is, being interpreted, Damsel, I say unto thee, arise. And straightway the damsel arose, and walked; for she was of the age of twelve years. And they were astonished with a great astonishment. And he charged them straitly that no man should know it; and commanded that something should be given her to eat.

Mark 6:5-6

And he could there do no mighty work, save that he laid his hands upon a few sick folk, and healed them. And he marvelled because of their unbelief. And he went round about the villages, teaching.

Mark 6:53-56

And when they had passed over, they came into the land of Gennesaret, and drew to the shore.

And when they were come out of the ship, straightway they knew him, And ran through that whole region round about, and began to carry about in beds those that were sick, where they heard he was.

And whithersoever he entered, into villages, or cities, or country, they laid the sick in the streets, and besought him that they might touch if it were but the border of his garment: and as many as touched him were made whole.

Mark 10:46-52

And they came to Jericho: and as he went out of Jericho with his disciples and a great number of people, blind Bartimaeus, the son of Timaeus, sat by the highway side begging. And when he heard that it was Jesus of Nazareth, he began to cry out, and say, Jesus, thou Son of David, have mercy on me. And many charged him that he should hold his peace: but he cried the more a great deal, Thou Son of David, have mercy on me. And Jesus stood still, and commanded him to be called. And they call the blind man, saying unto him, Be of good

31

comfort, rise; he calleth thee. And he, casting away his garment, rose, and came to Jesus. And Jesus answered and said unto him, What wilt thou that I should do unto thee? The blind man said unto him, Lord, that I might receive my sight. And Jesus said unto him, Go thy way; thy faith hath made thee whole. And immediately he received his sight, and followed Jesus in the way.

Mark 11:22-24

And Jesus answering saith unto them, Have faith in God. For verily I say unto you, That whosoever shall say unto this mountain, Be thou removed, and be thou cast into the sea; and shall not doubt in his heart, but shall believe that those things which he saith shall come to pass; he shall have whatsoever he saith. Therefore I say unto you, What things soever ye desire, when ye pray, believe that ye receive them, and ye shall have them.

Mark 16:15-20

And he said unto them, Go ye into all the world, and preach the gospel to every creature. He that believeth and is baptized shall be saved; but he that believeth not shall be damned. And these signs shall follow them that believe; In my name shall they cast out devils; they shall speak with new tongues; They shall take up serpents; and if they drink any deadly thing, it shall not hurt them; they shall lay hands on the sick, and they shall recover. So then after the Lord had spoken unto them, he was received up into heaven, and sat on the right hand of God. And they went forth, and preached every where, the Lord working with them, and confirming the word with signs following. Amen.

Luke 4:16-21

And he came to Nazareth, where he had been brought up: and, as his custom was, he went into the synagogue on the Sabbath day, and stood up for to read. And there was delivered unto him the book of the prophet Esaias. And when he had opened the book, he found the place where it was written,

The Spirit of the Lord is upon me, because he hath anointed me to preach the gospel to the poor; he hath sent me to heal the brokenhearted, to preach deliverance to the captives, and recovering of sight to the blind, to set at liberty them that are bruised, To preach the acceptable year of the Lord. And he closed the book, and he gave it again to the minister, and sat down. And the eyes of all them that were in the synagogue were fastened on him. And he began to say unto them, This day is this scripture fulfilled in your ears.

Luke 4:40

Now when the sun was setting, all they that had any sick with divers diseases brought them unto him; and he laid his hands on every one of them, and healed them.

Luke 6:6-10

And it came to pass also on another Sabbath, that he entered into the synagogue and taught: and there was a man whose right hand was withered. And the scribes and Pharisees watched him, whether he would heal on the Sabbath day; that they might find an accusation against him. But he knew their thoughts, and said to the man which had the withered hand, Rise up, and stand forth in the midst. And he arose and stood forth. Then said Jesus unto them, I will ask you one thing; Is it lawful on the Sabbath days to do good, or to do evil? to save life, or to destroy it? And looking round about upon them all, he said unto the man, Stretch forth thy hand. And he did so: and his hand was restored whole as the other.

Luke 6:17-19

And he came down with them, and stood in the plain, and the company of his disciples, and a great multitude of people out of all Judaea and Jerusalem, and from the sea coast of Tyre and Sidon, which came to hear him, and to be healed of their diseases; And they that were vexed with unclean spirits: and they were healed. And the whole multitude sought to touch him: for there went virtue out of him, and healed them all.

Luke 7:1-3

Now when he had ended all his sayings in the audience of the people, he entered into Capernaum.

And a certain centurion's servant, who was dear unto him, was sick, and ready to die. And when he heard of Jesus, he sent unto him the elders of the Jews, beseeching him that he would come and heal his servant.

LUKE 7:4-17

And when they came to Jesus, they besought him instantly, saying, That he was worthy for whom he should do this: For he loveth our nation, and he hath built us a synagogue. Then Jesus went with them. And when he was now not far from the house, the centurion sent friends to him, saying unto him, Lord, trouble not thyself: for I am not worthy that thou shouldest enter under my roof: Wherefore neither thought I myself worthy to come unto thee: but say in a word, and my servant shall be healed. For I also am a man set under authority, having under me soldiers, and I say unto one, Go, and he goeth; and to another, Come, and he cometh; and to my servant, Do this, and he doeth it. When Jesus heard these things, he marvelled at him, and turned him about, and said unto the people that followed him, I say unto you, I have not found so great faith, no, not in Israel. And they that were sent, returning to the house, found the servant whole that had been sick. And it came to pass the day after, that he went into a city called Nain; and many of his disciples went with him, and much people. Now when he came nigh to the gate of the city, behold, there was a dead man carried out, the only son of his mother, and she was a widow: and much people of the city was with her. And when the Lord saw her, he had compassion on her, and said unto her, Weep not. And he came and touched the bier: and they that bare him stood still. And he said, Young man, I say unto thee, Arise. And he that was dead sat up, and began to speak. And he delivered him to his mother. And there came a fear on all: and they glorified God, saying, That a great prophet is risen up among us; and, That God hath visited his people. And this rumour of him went forth throughout all Judaea, and throughout all the region round about.

Luke 9:1-2, 6, 11

Then he called his twelve disciples together, and gave them power and authority over all devils, and to cure diseases. And he sent them to preach the kingdom of God, and to heal the sick.

And they departed, and went through the towns, preaching the gospel, and healing every where.

And the people, when they knew it, followed him: and he received them, and spake unto them of the kingdom of God, and healed them that had need of healing. **(AMPLIFIED)** Then Jesus called together the Twelve [apostles] and gave them power and authority over all demons, and to cure diseases. And He sent them out to announce and preach the kingdom of God and to bring healing. And departing, they went about from village to village, preaching the Gospel and restoring the afflicted to health everywhere. But when the crowds learned of it, [they] followed Him; and He welcomed them and talked to them about the kingdom of God, and healed those who needed restoration to health.

Luke 10:8-9

And into whatsoever city ye enter, and they receive you, eat such things as are set before you:

And heal the sick that are therein, and say unto them, The kingdom of God is come nigh unto you.

Luke 18:35-43

And it came to pass, that as he was come nigh unto Jericho, a certain blind man sat by the way side begging: And hearing the multitude pass by, he asked what it meant. And they told him, that Jesus of Nazareth passeth by. And he cried, saying, Jesus, thou son of David, have mercy on me. And they which went before rebuked him, that he should hold his peace: but he cried so much the more, Thou son of David, have mercy on me. And Jesus stood, and commanded him to be brought unto him: and when he was come near, he asked him, Saying, What wilt thou that I shall do unto thee? And he said, Lord, that I may receive my sight. And Jesus said unto him, Receive thy sight: thy faith hath saved thee. And immediately he received his sight, and followed him, glorifying God: and all the people, when they saw it, gave praise unto God. **(AMPLIFIED)** As He came near to Jericho, it occurred that a blind man was sitting by the roadside begging. And hearing a crowd going by, he asked what it meant. They told him, Jesus of Nazareth is passing by. And he shouted, saying, Jesus, Son of David, take pity and have mercy on me! But those who were in front reproved him, telling him to keep quiet; yet he screamed and shrieked so much the more, Son of David, take pity and have mercy on me! Then Jesus stood still and ordered that he be led to Him; and when he came near, Jesus asked him, What do you want Me to do for you? He said, Lord, let me receive my sight! And Jesus said to him, Receive your sight! Your faith (your trust and confidence that spring from your faith in God) has healed you. And instantly he received his sight and began to follow Jesus, recognizing, praising, and honoring God; and all the people, when they saw it, praised God.

John 10:10

The thief cometh not, but for to steal, and to kill, and to destroy: I am come that they might have life, and that they might have it more abundantly.

John 14:13-14

And whatsoever ye shall ask in my name, that will I do, that the Father may be glorified in the Son.

If ye shall ask any thing in my name, I will do it.

John 15:7

If ye abide in me, and my words abide in you, ye shall ask what ye will, and it shall be done unto you.

John 16:23-24

And in that day ye shall ask me nothing. Verily, verily, I say unto you, Whatsoever ye shall ask the Father in my name, he will give it you. Hitherto have ye asked nothing in my name: ask, and ye shall receive, that your joy may be full.

Acts 10:38

How God anointed Jesus of Nazareth with the Holy Ghost and with power: who went about doing good, and healing all that were oppressed of the devil; for God was with him.

Acts 14:8-10

And there sat a certain man at Lystra, impotent in his feet, being a cripple from his mother's womb, who never had walked: The same heard Paul speak: who stedfastly beholding him, and perceiving that he had faith to be healed, Said with a loud voice, Stand upright on thy feet. And he leaped and walked.

Romans 4:16-21

Therefore it is of faith, that it might be by grace; to the end the promise might be sure to all the seed; not to that only which is of the law, but to that also which is of the faith of Abraham; who is the father of us all, (As it is written, I have made thee a father of many nations,) before him whom he believed, even God, who quickeneth the dead, and calleth those things which be not as though they were.

Who against hope believed in hope, that he might become the father of many nations, according to that which was spoken, So shall thy seed be. And being not weak in faith, he considered not his own body now dead, when he was about an hundred years old, neither yet the deadness of Sarah's womb: He staggered not at the promise of God through unbelief; but was strong in faith, giving glory to God;

And being fully persuaded that, what he had promised, he was able also to perform.

Romans 8:2

For the law of the Spirit of life in Christ Jesus hath made me free from the law of sin and death.

Romans 8:11

But if the Spirit of him that raised up Jesus from the dead dwell in you, he that raised up Christ from the dead shall also quicken your mortal bodies by his Spirit that dwelleth in you. **(AMPLIFIED)** And if the Spirit of Him Who raised up Jesus from the dead dwells in you, [then] He Who raised up Christ Jesus from the dead will also restore to life your mortal (short-lived, perishable) bodies through His Spirit Who dwells in you.

Romans 8:32

He that spared not his own Son, but delivered him up for us all, how shall he not with him also freely give us all things? **(AMPLIFIED)** He who did not withhold or spare [even] His own Son but gave Him up for us all, will He not also with Him freely and graciously give us all [other] things?

1 Corinthians 6:20

For ye are bought with a price: therefore glorify God in your body, and in your spirit, which are God's.

1 Corinthians 12:7-11

But the manifestation of the Spirit is given to every man to profit withal. For to one is given by the Spirit the word of wisdom; to another the word of knowledge by the same Spirit; To another faith by the same Spirit; to another the gifts of healing by the same Spirit; To another the working of miracles; to another prophecy; to another discerning of spirits; to another divers kinds of tongues; to another the interpretation of tongues:

But all these worketh that one and the selfsame Spirit, dividing to every man severally as he will.

1 Corinthians 12:28

And God hath set some in the church, first apostles, secondarily prophets, thirdly teachers, after that miracles, then gifts of healings, helps, governments, diversities of tongues.

2 Corinthians 10:3-5

For though we walk in the flesh, we do not war after the flesh: (For the weapons of our warfare are not carnal, but mighty through God to the pulling down of strong holds;) Casting down imaginations, and every high thing that exalteth itself against the knowledge of God, and bringing into captivity every thought to the obedience of Christ;

Galatians 3:13-14, 29

Christ hath redeemed us from the curse of the law, being made a curse for us: for it is written, Cursed is every one that hangeth on a tree: That the blessing of Abraham might come on the Gentiles through Jesus Christ; that we might receive the promise of the Spirit through faith.

And if ye be Christ's, then are ye Abraham's seed, and heirs according to the promise.

Ephesians 6:10-17

Finally, my brethren, be strong in the Lord, and in the power of his might. Put on the whole armour of God, that ye may be able to stand against the wiles of the devil. For we wrestle not against flesh and blood, but against principalities, against powers, against the rulers of the darkness of this world, against spiritual wickedness in high places. Wherefore take unto you the whole armour of God, that ye may be able to withstand in the evil day, and having done all, to stand. Stand therefore, having your loins girt about with truth, and having on the breastplate of righteousness; And your feet shod with the preparation of the gospel of peace; Above all, taking the shield of faith, wherewith ye shall be able to quench all the fiery darts of the wicked. And take the helmet of salvation, and the sword of the Spirit, which is the word of God:

Philippians 2:13

For it is God which worketh in you both to will and to do of his good pleasure.

Philippians 4:6-7

Be careful for nothing; but in every thing by prayer and supplication with thanksgiving let your requests be made known unto God. And the peace of God, which passeth all understanding, shall keep your hearts and minds through Christ Jesus.

2 Timothy 1:7

For God hath not given us the spirit of fear; but of power, and of love, and of a sound mind.

(AMPLIFIED) For God did not give us a spirit of timidity (of cowardice, of craven and cringing and fawning fear), but [He has given us a spirit] of power and of love and of calm and well-balanced mind and discipline and self control.

Hebrews 2:14-15

Forasmuch then as the children are partakers of flesh and blood, he also himself likewise took part of the same; that through death he might destroy him that had the power of death, that is, the devil;

And deliver them who through fear of death were all their lifetime subject to bondage.

Hebrews 10:23

Let us hold fast the profession of our faith without wavering; (for he is faithful that promised;)

(AMPLIFIED) So let us seize and hold fast and retain without wavering the hope we cherish and confess and our acknowledgement of it, for He Who promised is reliable (sure) and faithful to His word.

Hebrews 10:35-36

Cast not away therefore your confidence, which hath great recompence of reward.

For ye have need of patience, that, after ye have done the will of God, ye might receive the promise.

(AMPLIFIED) Do not, therefore, fling away your fearless confidence, for it carries a great and glorious compensation of reward. For you have need of steadfast patience, and endurance, so that you may perform and fully accomplish the will of God, and thus receive and carry away [and enjoy to the full] what is promised.

Hebews 11:1, 6, 11

Now faith is the substance of things hoped for, the evidence of things not seen.

But without faith it is impossible to please him: for he that cometh to God must believe that he is, and that he is a rewarder of them that diligently seek him.

Through faith also Sara herself received strength to conceive seed, and was delivered of a child when she was past age, because she judged him faithful who had promised.

Hebrews 13:8

Jesus Christ the same yesterday, and today, and for ever.

James 1:17

Every good gift and every perfect gift is from above, and cometh down from the Father of lights, with whom is no variableness, neither shadow of turning.

James 5:14-16

Is any sick among you? let him call for the elders of the church; and let them pray over him, anointing him with oil in the name of the Lord: And the prayer of faith shall save the sick, and the Lord shall raise him up; and if he have committed sins, they shall be forgiven him. Confess your faults one to another, and pray one for another, that ye may be healed. The effectual fervent prayer of a righteous man availeth much.

1 Peter 2:24

Who his own self bare our sins in his own body on the tree, that we, being dead to sins, should live unto righteousness: by whose stripes ye were healed.

I John 3:21-22

Beloved, if our heart condemn us not, then have we confidence toward God. And whatsoever we ask, we receive of him, because we keep his commandments, and do those things that are pleasing in his sight.

I John 5:14-15

And this is the confidence that we have in him, that, if we ask any thing according to his will, he heareth us: And if we know that he hear us, whatsoever we ask, we know that we have the petitions that we desired of him.

III John 1:2

Beloved, I wish above all things that thou mayest prosper and be in health, even as thy soul prospereth. **(AMPLIFIED)** Beloved, I pray that you may prosper in every way and [that your body] may keep well, even as [I know] your soul keeps well and prospers.

TESTIMONY TIME

Revelations 12:11 (Amplified) says, "And they have overcome (conquered) him by means of the blood of the Lamb and by the utterance of their testimony…" Enclosed you will find inspiring, uplifting and life changing testimonies from various people. I pray that you will enjoy reading them as much as I have.

Be blessed.

Testimony #1

I wanted to share my testimony with you, as it is very important to me, and I hope it will perhaps strengthen other's faith in Our Lord, Jesus Christ. Because through all of this- I learned that The Lord God has ultimate control over our lives. If we will <u>allow</u> Him to rule…He will. I am reminded of this, every day that I wake up. And for that, I am forever grateful!

Our Lord is amazing and every day I grow closer to Him and realize what a joy it truly is to have Him rule over your own life. The story I am about to share with you will show you how controlling He actually is and that He does rule, not only in your heart if you allow Him to, but also your life. You see, I am one who is known to be controlling. By that, I mean that I am responsible for everything in my life and everything that I do. I expect nothing but love from my family and friends. If there is ever anything that I want or need to be completed- I simply do it myself. Whatever it takes- I do it. Especially, if I want something done right (in my eyes)- I simply do it myself. I ask nothing from anyone except what I am willing to give and only, only, only if I really need help, do I even ask. Which isn't very often. I am very independent and do everything on my own. I am proud to say that I make what I feel to be very admirable choices in life and am proud of it.

So, now that you know me briefly, you can imagine that I have a tough time *"turning things over"* to The Lord. Please don't misunderstand me...I pray about things constantly. I pray that I will make the right choice...I pray that God will give me the knowledge to make the best, most logical choice according to His will...I pray that God will show me His way. But I do pray that **"I"** will make the right choice. That **I, I, I** will make the right choice. How often do we pray about things and give them to The Lord...only to take them back shortly after praying about them and take it upon ourselves to make the choice instead of allowing God to do so? I found myself doing this quite often and missing what God really had to offer me. I would take control and try to make, what seemed like, the best decision.

Well, I was missing the boat! Here's why. I decided last January that I would go to school and obtain my real estate license. I wanted extra money to pay a few extra bills off. I certainly didn't want to make a career out of it. That is too scary. After all, I had been working in the corporate world for nearly 8 years. Plus, my mom worked at the company as well as my husband. I enjoyed being with them every day and had no notion to leave. Plus, working in real estate means you learn to work when everybody else is off – which means you had to work weekends. I am one that enjoys playing hard and wasn't willing to give up my weekends. I never entertained the thought- much at all! Getting my license wasn't easy. But I knew that if I set my mind to it- I could do it. So, soon after my marriage- I begin school to learn real estate. I completed a 6-month program in only 3 months. I somehow, by the grace of God, managed to be a newlywed wife, a mother of a 6 week old puppy, a full time employee and a part time student….and still remained married once it was all completed. Time for the finals rolled around and I passed!!! Now, that alone was a prayer answered because I am the worst test taker on the face of the planet. Proof of that are my 4 attempts at passing the GRE to go back to school to complete my masters program. I failed all four times.

My scores were never high enough to get into any Georgia university- no matter my preparation. I am terrible at passing exams. But- I successfully passed both of these and on the first attempt! I did a lot of praying, believe me.

So, I fiddle through the paper work and now it's April and I have my license. Wow. What now? We took a vacation and upon our return I began researching real estate companies. I knew from the beginning that I would go with the company, Remax Advantage- because that is where my builder's license was held. Plus, he had tried several times to convince me to come to work for him there. He continued to support me and show me how much money is available to be made. I listened to him and joined Remax part time. I began showing houses the second week of June. I immediately got a "listing" on a house-, which brought me even more buyers to work with. All this time- praying that God will help show me the way. Show me and help me to know if this job was right for me. He sent me my answer. He sent it loud and clear. In a matter of weeks- I had 6 contracts written all to close beginning July 21st through August 31st. **Six closings within a month and ½.** That totaled about $8,000 extra monies for my husband and me. Once my "beginner's fees/ one time fees" were extracted- I was left with about $5,000. Everybody in my immediate office was shocked. I was shocked. I prayed for God's wisdom and guidance and the ability to work with other people. I prayed that people would trust me and see the good that I had to offer. I allowed Him to have control over my life and He did. I feel like He opened doors for me.

My builder, still in shock, asks me to work for him full time. He offered me the ultimate gift, which is a sub-division and wanted me to work for him immediately. I kept telling him no. I told him that I really needed my full time position and couldn't give up the guaranteed money. Besides- I really enjoyed making an extra $8,000 for one months worth of work. I explained that I was too worried about money to quit my job. Instead- I would just work late hours and on the weekends in addition to my regular job just to make sure things got done. You see- I knew that **I** had things under control. I recognized that I would have to simply work harder to make things happen. I could do it. I could do it on my own, just fine. Sure, The Lord had opened some doors- but He meant for me to keep running through them as quickly as I could. Right? With my personality- I can do it......so I thought. In a matter of a month- I went from healthy to not so healthy. My blood pressure became high and I experienced what the doctor called, anxiety attacks. I began to realize that maybe I can't do this on my own. Perhaps the control that I thought I had over the situation wasn't that at all. I began praying and praying and asking My God to show me His way. I explained that I couldn't go on like this. I cried for Him to help show me what His/my decision should be. That very next weekend, my real-estate boss offered me "whatever it takes to get you here full time". He told me to name my price. I explained that I needed my car paid off and two credit card bills which all totaled an additional $7,000. He wrote me a check, on the spot. I couldn't believe what I was seeing. He told me to consider it a "signing bonus". There was my answer. God had made it possible for it to happen. My boss believed in me so much that he was willing to come out of pocket for that amount of money to have me their full time. He said that I would make him and myself more money than I can imagine but on a more flexible schedule. God had answered my prayers. He had taken control over something that I couldn't possibly control myself. I went to the doctor yesterday for my follow up appointment and my blood pressure was normal. No medications needed and no anxiety felt. What a truly magnificent God He is and what a wonderful lesson I learned. Trust and love your God and let Him have control over your life. It's the only way

R.W.-ATLANTA, GA.

Testimony #2

I had been believing God for a promotion. I knew that I had worked hard, and felt that I was deserving of one; however, thoughts kept coming to my mind telling me not to build myself up for one because I would be disappointed if it did not happen. I also kept focusing on whether or not different people would impact whether or not I received the promotion.

I was watching a World Changers Ministry broadcast one morning, and a young lady was giving her testimony. She said that she had been confessing for a promotion. She said that she just used the words that "I will get a promotion" over and over again. She said that Pastor Dollar taught that you need to use God's word when you are confessing. She mentioned that she starting confessing Psalms 75:6-7 which says, "For promotion cometh neither from the east, nor from the west, nor from the south. But God is the judge: he putteth down one, and setteth up another." I knew **that** word was for me. From that point, it became my confession. Instead of worrying about a promotion, I had perfect peace.

Since I had peace in that area, Satan tried to disturb my peace. A day before I was to have my annual review with my manager, I received a call from my son's doctor. Although it had only happened once, she was concerned that blood was in his urine, and wanted to have his kidneys checked. I scheduled the test, but immediately began confessing healing scriptures over my son.

The next day, I had my review. My manager told me that I would receive a promotion. **ALL PRAISE, GLORY, AND HONOR TO THE MOST HIGH GOD.** As soon as I received my promotion, I had total peace about my son just by seeing how faithful God was in promoting me, and by knowing that "his word does not return unto him void." My son had the test. It has been 2 weeks since the test, and we have not received a final report. I talked to the nurse, and she told me that had the radiologist found anything, that his doctor would have been contacted. That was confirmation for me for what I already knew – "that by Jesus stripes, he was healed."

D. J.-ATLANTA, GA.

Testimony #3

About a month ago my husband and I started noticing some swelling around our daughter Sierra's eyes. At first we thought she had somehow gotten into something that got in her eyes. At her 15-month checkup, I mentioned the swelling to her doctor who said that maybe it was something that she had eaten to which she could be allergic.

Well, Chris (my husband) and I just prayed over her because we had no idea what it could be. We tried eliminating certain foods to see if maybe that was it. At one point, we thought it might be the new body spray we purchased. No matter what we eliminated, the swelling did not disappear. It would switch from eye to eye.

We were praying and believing God for her healing no matter what the cause, but we still wanted to find out what exactly was causing the swelling. About a week ago, I took her in to get some testing done, and the doctor prescribed some eye drops, and also some type of steroid to cause the swelling to go down. Two days later, the doctor called me while I was at work to say that the blood test results didn't look good at all, and that they needed for us to take Sierra to Scottish Rite Children's Hospital right away for an ultrasound to determine whether or not her kidneys were functioning properly.

Well, my first thought was to be emotionally upset, but I then recalled what the Word of God had to say about healing in Isaiah 53:5, and 1 Peter 2:24 and I told my mind that it had to line up with that Word. I began to speak faith-filled words to that fear, and made a decision to believe God's report over whatever the test results were. To make a long story short, Chris never wavered in his belief that God had already taken care of whatever it was, and I prayed and spoke the Word in 16-month old Sierra's little ear. With all the test results in, her kidneys and all her other organs are 100% healthy. She was just in need of some iron supplement drops and her eyes are now back to normal!

My husband Chris and I have no doubt in our minds that the Lord healed Sierra, and had we given into the fear that Satan was trying to instill in us, her diagnosis would have been much worse. **PRAISE GOD FOR BEING JEHOVAH-RAPHA** in our lives today!

T.C.-ATLANTA, GA.

Testimony #4

One Friday afternoon, I received a call from my son who was at school. He said that when he woke up from a short nap after lunch, he was unable to see clearly. He could only see a large white image. I immediately took him to the doctor's office. A vision test was done. It indicated that he had 20/100 vision in both eyes.

His doctor examined him thoroughly. She could not find anything out of the ordinary. She called a neurologist who mentioned there could be a number of things causing the problem. I was told to take my son to the emergency room of the Children's hospital. His eyes were examined in the emergency room. His vision test indicated that he had 20/70 vision in 1 eye, and 20/50 vision in the other eye. They even checked to make sure his eyeball had not been scratched. It had not.

The emergency room contacted an Ophthalmologist. We were told that my son needed to see him the following day. From the very moment that my son called me and stated the problem he was having, I kept confessing healing scriptures. I told him to do the same. **I did not get upset. I trusted God to do what his word said**. Before my son went to bed, I told him to confess that he had 20/20 vision.

The next day, the Ophthalmologist ran a battery of vision tests. In listening to my son respond to the doctor's questions, my husband thought that he was not doing so well. When all of the tests had been done, the Ophthalmologist said that nothing was wrong with my son's eyes-that he had 20/20 vision. **ALL PRAISE, GLORY, AND HONOR TO THE MOST HIGH GOD!**

D.J.-ATLANTA, GA.

CONCLUSION

Now I would like to pray for you. *Father, in the Name of Jesus, I come before You, thanking You that your Word is true. I believe that as the children of God read and confess these scriptures, their bodies are being affected, right now, by the anointed Word of God. Father, I thank You that your Word has removed every symptom of sickness, disease and pain. Jesus, You are our healer and the healing power of God's Word is flowing through their bodies right now! Satan I command you to loose God's people! Take your hands off God's property. I declare that you have no authority, no power and no dominion. You are defeated, and the blood of Jesus is against you. I command every cell, nerve, organ, muscle, tissue, bone, immune system and every limb on their bodies to be made whole, and to function as God has created. Father, I give you thanks, right now, that it is done, in the Name of Jesus! Amen.*

God bless, and may you continue to walk in divine health.

Love,

Minister Leslie J. Kimbro

PRAYER FOR SALVATION

If you have not received Jesus as your personal Lord and Savior, please open your mouth and pray the following prayer:

Heavenly Father, I come to you in the name of Jesus. Your Word says in Acts 2:21 "that whosoever shall call on the name of the Lord shall be saved." I am calling on you. I pray and ask Jesus to come into my heart and be Lord over my life according to Romans 10:9,10: "If thou shalt confess with thou mouth and believe in thine heart that God hath raised him from the dead, thou shalt be saved." I do that now. I confess that Jesus is Lord, and I believe in my heart that God hath raised Him from the dead.

I am now born again!

I am a Christian — a child of the Almighty God!

I am saved.

If you prayed that prayer and made Jesus the Lord of your life, please write, send an e-mail, or call our ministry office. We would like to send you a packet called *The Next Steps*. This information is free of charge.

Minister Leslie J. Kimbro

Daily Living In The Word Of God Ministries, Inc.

P.O. Box 310959

Atlanta, GA 31131-0959

Phone: (404) 763-1313

E-mail: <u>godfirst@bellsouth.net</u>

www.godfirst.com

TAPES AVAILABLE BY MINISTER LESLIE J. KIMBRO

Tape Titles	Item #	Price
Tape Albums		
Do you want to be made well? (3-tape album)	A 01-003	$15.00
How to Maintain my Healing (2-tape album)	A 01-004	$10.00
Divine Health Can Be Yours (Int'l Healing Sch)	A 01-005	$65.00
Whose Money is it Anyway? (3-tape album)	A 01-006	$15.00
Single Audio Cassettes		
The Power of Words	S 01-001	$5.00
How to Maintain the Glow in Adverse Circumstances	S 01-002	$5.00
Why Should I Tithe and Give Offerings	S 01-003	$5.00

Spending Time With the One You Love	S 01-004	$5.00
Expectation-Having an Expectant Heart	S 01-005	$5.00
Why Confession?	S 01-006	$5.00
Pray what the Word Says	S 01-007	$5.00
How to Resist Satan at all Times	S 01-008	$5.00
How to Take God's Medicine	S 01-009	$5.00
God's Precious Promises on Healing	S 01-010	$5.00
Road Blocks that will Hinder Your Healing	S 01-011	$5.00
Faith and Medicine Work Together	S 01-012	$5.00
Covenant of Healing & Becoming Aggressive to Receive	S 01-013	$5.00

Use Faith to Get Healed	S 01-014	$5.00
Don't Quit, Your Faith will See You Through!	S 01-015	$5.00
Fruit of the Spirit (Patience) Longsuffering	S 01-016	$5.00
The Covenant of Wealth	S 01-017	$5.00
How to Honor God with the Tithe	S 01-018	$5.00
What is the Offering For?	S 01-019	$5.00
Maintaining Dominion Without Compromising the Kingdom	S 01-020	$5.00
Developing a Servant's Heart	S 01-021	$5.00
The Righteousness Of God (Healing Sch Version)	S 01-022	$5.00
We Are The Righteousness Of God	S 01-023	$5.00
Abiding In His Presence	S 01-024	$5.00

Please complete and mail the enclosed order form to the ministry office along with a check or money order.

Thank you for your order!

TAPE ORDER FORM

Daily Living In The Word Of God Ministries, Inc.

Minister Leslie J. Kimbro

"But seek ye first the kingdom of God, and His righteousness and all these things shall be added unto you." (Matthew 6:33)

DATE:_____

Mail To:

Name_____

Address_____

City,   State,

Zip_____

Leslie J. Kimbro

Quantity	Item #	Teaching Title	Unit Price	Amount

Subtotal $_____

Contribution $_____

Total Enclosed $_____

Please make all checks or money orders payable to:

Daily Living In The Word Of God Ministries, Inc. or DLWGM
(Charges include shipping and handling).

Please mail order form to:

DLWGM

P.O. Box 310959

Atlanta, GA. 31131-0959

THANK YOU FOR YOUR SUPPORT OF DAILY LIVING IN THE WORD OF GOD MINISTRIES, INC.

Satisfaction Guaranteed

JESUS IS LORD!

ABOUT THE AUTHOR

Minister Kimbro is the anointed Founder and President of *Daily Living In The Word Of God Ministries, Inc.,* a non-profit outreach ministry in Atlanta, Georgia. She is an ordained Minister of the Gospel who has a passion for God's people and a desire to truly operate in the gifts and callings of God, unto His glory.

Embracing her commission from God to teach His children to develop a personal relationship with Jesus Christ (while teaching Believers to use their God-given authority), Minister Kimbro also conducts Healing School classes through her ministry. These classes are taught twice a month, and have been a powerful force in the lives of many who made a quality decision to receive God's blessings by way of His healing power.

Minister Kimbro is a native of Philadelphia, PA. She, her husband Curtis, their son Curtis Sims

Kimbro, daughter-in-law Nasheekah and grandson "CJ", live in Atlanta, Georgia. She is affiliated with many area churches, and is a partner with several worldwide ministries.

For speaking engagements or information, please call (404) 763-1313, or send e-mail to godfirst@bellsouth.net. Please visit our web site at www.godfirst.com.

Daily Living In The Word Of God Ministries, Inc., is built on:

> *Integrity*
> *Excellence*
> *Faith*